Nashua Public Library

Enjoy this book!
Please remember to return it on time
so that others may enjoy it too.

Manage your library account and
discover all we offer by visiting us
online at www.nashualibrary.org

Love your library? Tell a friend!

J

LIFE IN MEDIEVAL EUROPE

THE COUNTRYSIDE IN MEDIEVAL EUROPE

DANIELLE WATSON

Cavendish
Square

New York

A portion of the material in this book has been derived from *Everyday Life in Medieval Europe* by Kathryn Hinds.

Published in 2017 by Cavendish Square Publishing, LLC
243 5th Avenue, Suite 136, New York, NY 10016

Library of Congress Cataloging-in-Publication Data

Names: Watson, Danielle, 1978-
Title: The countryside in medieval Europe / Danielle Watson.
Description: New York : Cavendish Square Publishing, 2017. |
Series: Life in medieval Europe | Includes bibliographical references and index. |
Description based on print version record and CIP data provided by publisher; resource not viewed.
Identifiers: LCCN 2016000359 (print) | LCCN 2015050692 (ebook) |
ISBN 9781502618832 (ebook) | ISBN 9781502618825 (library bound)
Subjects: LCSH: Country life--Europe--History--To 1500--Juvenile literature. |
Villages--Europe--History--To 1500--Juvenile literature. |
Civilization, Medieval--Juvenile literature. | Europe--Social life and customs--Juvenile literature. |
Europe--History--476-1492--Juvenile literature.
Classification: LCC CB353 (print) | LCC CB353 .W36 2017 (ebook) |
DDC 909.07--dc23
LC record available at http://lccn.loc.gov/2016000359

Editorial Director: David McNamara
Editor: Kelly Spence
Copy Editor: Nathan Heidelberger
Art Director: Jeffrey Talbot
Designer: Joseph Macri
Production Assistant: Karol Szymczuk
Photo Research: J8 Media

Contents

THE MEDIEVAL AGE

The work of a medieval village took place year-round. In this illustration from the 1500s, peasants chop and gather wood to stoke their fires during the cold winter months.

The medieval period, also known as the Middle Ages, spans about one thousand years of European history, between 500 and 1500. The years 1100–1400 made up the High Middle Ages, a period distinguished by a swelling population that led to great social, economic, and political changes across the continent.

The late Middle Ages saw the emergence of **humanists**, individuals who, during the fourteenth century, took a renewed interest in ancient Roman and Greek literature and ideologies. Humanists believed that the previous ten centuries had been a dark age, with no great human advancements or thinkers. They sought to distance themselves from this time period and to create a rebirth of ancient learning. The rise of humanism led to the period following the Middle Ages, which became known as the Renaissance.

During the Middle Ages, about 90 percent of people lived in small, tightly knit villages scattered across the European countryside. These village dwellers were predominantly peasants who farmed the land and raised livestock. These rural communities formed an integral part of medieval society, providing food to most people, from lowly beggars to powerful kings and nobles.

CHAPTER ONE

A DIVIDED SOCIETY

During the month of September, medieval peasants harvest grapes. Much of the crop would then be aged and made into wine.

"It is the custom in England, as in other countries, for the nobility to have great power over the common people, who are their serfs. This means that they are bound by law and custom to plough the field of their masters, harvest the corn, gather it into barns, and thresh and winnow the grain; they must also mow and carry home the hay, cut and collect wood, and perform all manner of tasks of this kind."

—Jean Froissart writing on the role
of the medieval peasant, 1395

From wealthy lords to lowly **serfs**, medieval society was largely divided. Power was hierarchical, with the king holding the most power. Power then filtered down to noble lords, who oversaw medieval **manors** on which peasants worked to farm the land and raise livestock.

A noble's lord was either a more powerful noble or a king. The lord granted land and gave protection to the lower-ranking noble, called a **vassal**. In return, the vassal pledged loyalty and obedience to the lord, particularly promising to fight for the lord in battle during times of war. This military and political arrangement, which developed in the early Middle Ages, is known as **feudalism** (FYOO-duh-lizm).

Older history books often described feudalism as the social system of medieval Europe. It was thought that there was a feudal "chain of command" that stretched from the mightiest king down to the lowliest peasant. More recently, though, historians have concluded that feudal relationships affected only the top levels of medieval society, made up of kings and nobles.

The peasants, who made up the majority of medieval Europeans, were not part of this feudal network, which depended on military service and personal vows of loyalty. The relationship between peasants and their lords, often called **manorialism**, was different. Manorialism was the basic economic system in much of Europe until the late Middle Ages. As in feudalism, this system

The Domesday Book

In 1066, William the Conqueror became the new king of England. The new king gave power over many areas to his Norman friends. By 1085, disputes were arising between these lords. The king sent his men out to take a survey of his domain. He wanted to know the total value of his kingdom and figure out ways he could grow his wealth by increasing taxes.

To collect this information, the king's men went out to all corners of the kingdom. A modern English translation from the Domesday Book describes the standard questions asked by the king's officials at each manor:

> They inquired what the manor was called; who held it at the time of King
> Edward; who holds it now; how many hides [land equaling between 60 and
> 120 acres, or 24 to 48 hectares] there are; how many ploughs in **demesne** [held
> by the lord] and how many belonging to the men; how many villagers; how many
> cottagers; how many slaves; how many freemen; how many **sokemen**; how much
> woodland; how much meadow; how much pasture; how many mills; how many
> fisheries; how much had been added to or taken away from the estate; what it
> used to be worth altogether; what it is worth now; and how much each freeman
> and sokeman had and has.

was based on exchange. Peasants expected protection from their lord and were granted land by him. Instead of military service, however, peasants gave the lord their labor and the products of their labor.

Manorialism was less common in some parts of Europe, such as Frisia (the modern-day Netherlands), Scandinavia, and Scotland. The structure of the manorial system also varied from place to place. Toward the end of the Middle Ages, peasants were able to pay money to their lord in place of working for him.

All this was to be recorded thrice, namely as it was in the time of King Edward, as it was when King William gave it, and as it is now. And it was also to be noted whether more could be taken than is now being taken.

Of the land surveyed, the royal family held 17 percent, members of the Catholic Church held 26 percent, and 190 vassals controlled the remained 54 percent. Female landowners were also recorded. More than thirteen thousand locations were surveyed and included in the book. The Domesday Book is the oldest surviving public record and has provided many historians with much of their knowledge on the inner workings of feudalism and manorialism.

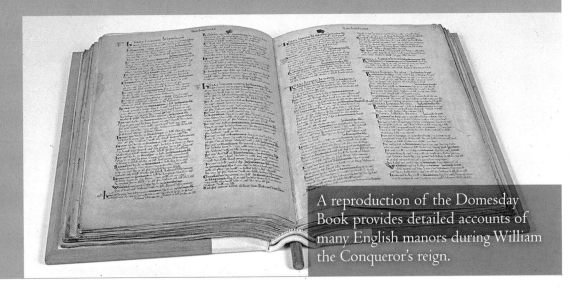

A reproduction of the Domesday Book provides detailed accounts of many English manors during William the Conqueror's reign.

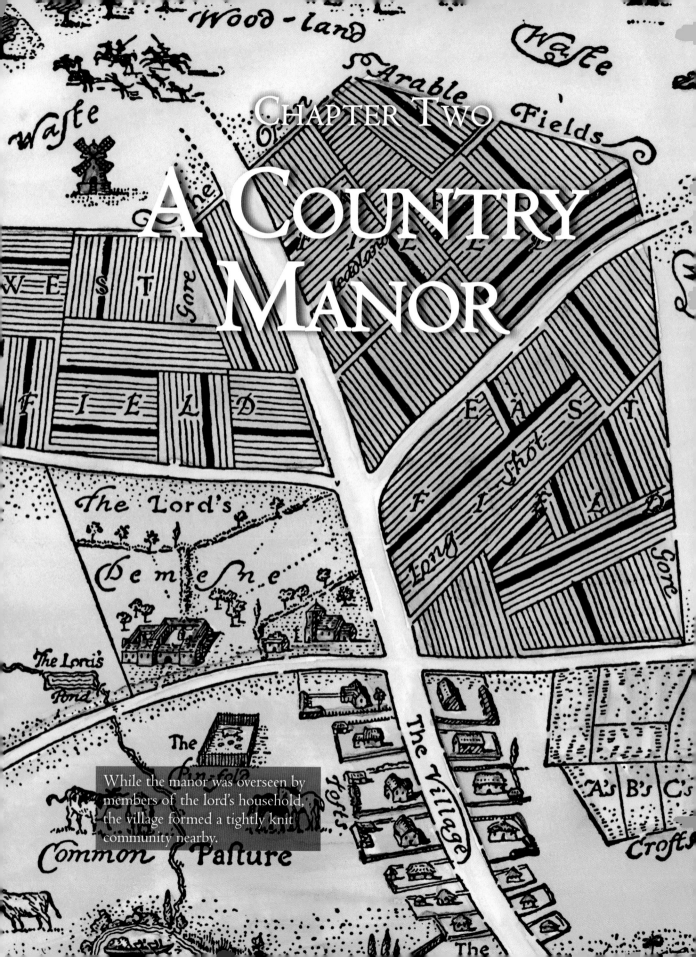

CHAPTER TWO

A COUNTRY MANOR

While the manor was overseen by members of the lord's household, the village formed a tightly knit community nearby.

"The steward ought … to cause all the demesne lands of each to be measured by true men, and he ought to know by the perch of the country how many acres there are in each field, and thereby he can know how much wheat, rye, barley, oats, peas, beans, and dredge one ought by right to sow in each acre, and thereby can one see if the provost or the hayward account for more seed than is right, and thereby can he see how many plows are required on the manor, for each plow ought by right to plow nine score acres, that is to say: sixty for winter seed, sixty for spring seed, and sixty in fallow."
—a description of a steward's duties in overseeing the lord's manor from 1295

A medieval manor consisted of many parts. At the center lay the manor house, where the lord and his family lived. Sprawling outward lay the lord's demesne (deh-MAIN), which was his own land, and land held by peasant villagers. In exchange for these plots of earth, the villagers owed the lord various services or payments. A single manor might be made up of part of a village, an entire village, or more than one village.

The lord of the manor was usually a nobleman, but not always. Sometimes the lord was a high-ranking church official, such as a bishop. Some manors were held by noble widows and heiresses. Other estates belonged to **abbeys**, religious communities for men or women. In such a case, the lord of the manor was the abbot or abbess who headed the community.

Some lords, such as low-ranking **knights** or nobles, held only one manor. Others—like the count of Champagne in what is now France—held dozens and were powerful enough to rival kings. Most lords held several manors, which were often widely scattered through the countryside. The lord might visit each manor in turn, or he might live at the court of his overlord or in one of Europe's growing cities. Usually the lord did not live year-round on any one manor, unless that was all he held.

Lords did not work the land themselves, so they depended on their estates to provide them with grain, meat, cheese, and most of the rest of the food for their households. The manors gave them beeswax for their candles and sheep's wool and sometimes linen for their clothes. Rents, fees, fines, and sales of extra produce from the manors provided lords with money for their other wants and needs.

Some lords preferred to lease out their estates; this practice was especially common during the 1100s. For a fixed fee, a lord would rent either the demesne or the entire manor to someone else. The renter then managed the property and was entitled to all the taxes and services that were owed to the lord. Usually the renter was another lord, a businessman from an area town, a knight, or a rich peasant. Sometimes a group of peasants who lived on the manor joined together to lease it.

Representatives of the Lord

Villagers rarely ever caught a glimpse of their lord. Typically, the lord did not run the manor himself. Instead, there were three main officials who oversaw the day-to-day workings of the manor. In England, these officials were known as the steward, the bailiff, and the reeve.

The steward (sometimes called a seneschal) was a knight or **cleric** who supervised all of the lord's manors, visiting each of them two or three times

A wood-cut reproduction of a medieval miniature shows peasants, ready with scythes in hand, receiving their daily tasks from the lord of the manor.

Laws of the Land

Court was held at certain times of the year. The manorial court served two main functions: to organize the logistics of running the manor and to punish individuals who broke the laws of the land. Local bylaws were written in the town's **custumal**. These laws restricted much of what a peasant could and could not do. For example, in one English town, a law ordered that before a peasant could put his pig out to pasture, he must pay a tax, called **pannage**. The fee was one penny per pig. If he was caught breaking this law, the peasant would lose his pig to the lord. Additionally, serfs could not leave the manor, learn to read or write, brew ale, or bake bread without the lord's permission.

The people who broke these laws, and the fines they paid, were recorded on manor rolls by the lord's court. On the manor, every person was made responsible for ensuring the laws were being followed by everyone else.

a year. The lord himself appointed the steward. One of the steward's most important duties when he was at a manor was to preside over the manorial court. Generally, all but the most serious crimes were tried in this court, which also settled disagreements between villagers and between villagers and the lord. Punishments from the manorial court were usually fines, which were paid to the lord.

The bailiff was the lord's representative on the manor. He was usually chosen by the steward. He might be a younger son from a noble family, or he might come from a well-to-do peasant family. In either case, he was expected to be able to read and write. His major responsibility was to manage the demesne, making sure that the lord's crops and livestock were properly taken care of. He also made sure that the manor had all the supplies it needed to function—everything from building materials to baskets. Anything that could not be produced on the manor itself had to be purchased in nearby towns. In addition, on many manors the bailiff was responsible for some aspects of law enforcement.

The reeve was a prosperous peasant who supervised the work for the lord. Usually the villagers elected him themselves. The reeve served a one-year term, though he could be reelected repeatedly. It was also his duty to keep the demesne's accounts. Throughout the year, he kept track of the villagers' workdays, the number of livestock, the size of the harvests, rents collected, and payments made. Since the reeve generally had no schooling and could neither read nor write, he recorded all these facts and figures by making marks on wooden tally sticks. At the end of the agricultural year (September 29 in England), he had to give a "reckoning" of the accounts to the steward or another official. The reeve was not paid for performing his office, but he was not required to do any other work for the lord.

Most manors also had a beadle, or hayward. This peasant assisted the reeve and was responsible for looking after the saving, storing, and sowing of the seeds for the demesne's grain crop. Other officers varied from estate to estate, but it seems that no manor, at least in England, was without ale tasters. These officials, who were often women, oversaw the quality and price of ale sold in the village. If they found that the ale was weak, its brewer had to pay the lord a fine.

Below the lord's representatives lay the working class, ranging from the town's merchants to the peasants bound to a lord and his land.

CHAPTER THREE

PARTS OF A MEDIEVAL VILLAGE

Houses showcasing the half-timber building style of many medieval homes dot the English countryside today.

"O my lord, I work very hard: I go out at dawn, driving
the cattle to the field, and I yoke them to the plow. Nor is
the weather so bad in winter that I dare to stay at home,
for fear of my lord: but when the oxen are yoked, and the
plowshare and coulter attached to the plow, I must plow
one whole field a day, or more."
—a plowman describes his workday in "The Dialogue
Between Master & Disciple:
On Laborers," circa 1000

Peasant houses and community buildings formed the tightly woven center of the medieval village. These buildings were surrounded by narrow fields of crops like grain, peas, and beans, which then gave way to meadows and woodlands on which livestock grazed.

Throughout much of western Europe, the village farmland was divided into three large fields. Peasant landholders had long strips of land in each, as long strips were easiest to plow. Every year, one field was left **fallow**, one was planted in the fall, and one was planted in the spring. Cattle, sheep, and horses were allowed to graze in the fields after the crops were harvested.

A Peasant House

Peasant dwellings ranged from tiny one-room cottages to high-ceilinged longhouses divided into four or five sections. They were not very solidly constructed—there are records of burglars easily smashing through a house's flimsy walls. Village houses often had to be rebuilt every thirty to forty years.

In England, each house had a yard, or **toft**, enclosed by a ditch or fence. A family might have storage sheds and other outbuildings in the toft. If the family had chickens, pigs, a cow, or an ox, the animals would have pens in the toft and would also graze there. Stretching back from the toft was the **croft**, a garden of about 0.5 acres (0.2 ha). This was where the family raised its vegetables. Some households also grew apple, pear, or cherry trees in the croft.

Often one end of the house had a byre, or barn, attached so that the family's livestock would be safe and sheltered during the winter. This was also beneficial to the family; the animals' body heat helped to keep the house warm. The other end might be partitioned off to form a storeroom.

The house's dirt floors were strewn with rushes, straw, or on special occasions, herbs and wildflowers. Usually there were only a few windows, which had shutters but no glass. In a typical longhouse there was a central hearth, where a fire burned all day long. A pot of porridge or pottage, a thick, hearty stew, usually could be found simmering over it. Since there was often no real chimney, the inside of the house was not only dim but also smoky.

Most families had little furniture. They ate meals at a trestle table—a board laid over supports—which was taken down every night. They sat on stools or benches. Instead of beds, most peasants slept on thin, straw-filled mattresses on the floor, sometimes in a loft at one end of the hall. Wooden chests were used to store blankets and clothes.

There was no bathroom, and no indoor plumbing at all. Usually one or two wells were shared by the entire village. Women and children had to fetch water from the well every day. Like most medieval Europeans, peasants bathed very

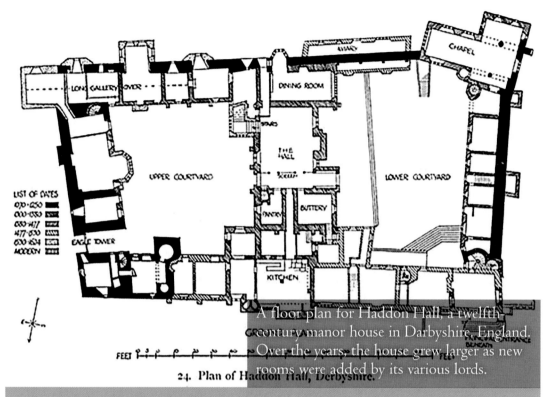

LIST OF DATES
070-1250
000-1330
030-1477
1477-1530
1530-1624
MODERN

LONG GALLERY OVER

DINING ROOM

CHAPEL

THE HALL

UPPER COURTYARD

LOWER COURTYARD

PANTRY

BUTTERY

EAGLE TOWER

KITCHEN

FEET

A floor plan for Haddon Hall, a twelfth-century manor house in Darbyshire, England. Over the years, the house grew larger as new rooms were added by its various lords.

24. Plan of Haddon Hall, Derbyshire.

The Manor House

If the village was part of more than one manor, it would probably have more than one manor house. Like the church, the manor house was built of stone, but it was much larger. It stood on 1 or 2 acres (0.4 or 0.8 ha) of ground and was often surrounded by a wall, fence, or moat. Within this enclosure, there were also likely to be stables, barns, **sheepfolds**, **dovecotes**, a chapel, a garden and orchard, a dairy, a kitchen, and a bakehouse.

The bailiff and his family lived in the manor house. This was also the place where royal messengers, high-ranking churchmen, friends and relatives of the lord, and other VIPs stayed when they visited the estate.

The most important feature of the manor house was the great hall, a huge, long, high-ceilinged room. In the great hall, guests were entertained, holidays were celebrated, and meetings were held. Above all, this was where the manorial court met.

rarely. When they did, the used a barrel with the top removed as a tub. Family members washed up one after the other, all using the same water. For other bathroom needs, most people simply went "a bowshot away" from the house, although some families dug a latrine trench in the yard.

SHARED SPACES

Along with the private houses, every village had some buildings that served the entire community. The church and the manor house were the most important of these.

Normally a village would have only one church (although some had none). The village church was usually a simple stone building. There were no benches or pews—worshipers had to sit on the floor, stand, or bring stools from home. Fancy stained-glass windows were probably rare in village churches, but the inside walls were often painted with biblical scenes. A favorite scene was the Last Judgment, showing God deciding who would be eternally rewarded and who would be eternally punished at the end of time.

Just outside was the churchyard, which included the village cemetery. Villagers often held dances and other festivities in the churchyard. Many priests disapproved of this, but some joined right in.

Other shared spaces provided villagers with their basic needs for living off and farming the land. To grind their grain, a villager would visit the mill; to bake their bread, the shared oven or bakehouse; and to obtain iron tools or horseshoes, the blacksmith at his forge. Many of these buildings were constructed around a central village green, which was used for grazing livestock and commonly as the site of public punishments for those who broke the village laws.

Harnessing Power

Grain was the basis of the peasant diet. It could be boiled to make porridge and gruel, or ground into flour to make bread. In northern Europe, before the Middle

A powerful wooden waterwheel saved a peasant much of the backbreaking work of grinding grain into flour.

Ages, grain was usually ground in stone querns, or hand mills. The ancient Romans generally used large millstones turned by donkeys or slaves. Yet the Romans knew of a better technology, the waterwheel, which probably originated in Persia or India. Mysteriously, the Romans rarely used the waterwheel.

In the early Middle Ages, however, western Europeans realized the great potential of the waterwheel. By the eleventh century, water-powered mills were grinding grain into flour all over Europe—wherever there was a fast-running stream to turn the mill's waterwheel. The wheel turned a pair of gears, which turned the millstone. Large amounts of grain could now be ground with very little effort.

Toward the end of the twelfth century, a new European invention made still more progress in the technology of grinding grain. This was the vertical windmill, probably developed in eastern England. Nothing like it had ever been seen before, but it was soon in use throughout western Europe. It caught the force of the wind in its sails, and their turning ran the gears that turned the millstone, grinding grain with little human effort.

The waterwheel and the windmill are examples of medieval Europe's search for new forms of nonhuman power and new ways to use it. Such technological advances pointed the way to even greater progress in the future. Great advances were also made with farming equipment, allowing peasants to till the land much faster and improve the yield of his or her harvest.

CHAPTER FOUR
VILLAGE LIFE

Wharram Percy is one of the best-preserved medieval villages in Britain. The remnants of over thirty peasant cottages, the church, and the manor house remain. This painting by British artist Peter Dunn depicts how the bustling village may have appeared during the Middle Ages.

"West Row and North Row were probably tenanted by villeins, while East Row comprises smaller, less regular plots that may have been occupied by cottars, who held no land other than their tofts. West Row is less obviously planned and may have been occupied by sokemen. It contains several larger longhouses ... which had a "cruck" timber frame and—unusually—glazed windows."
—a description of how the peasant homes were laid out in the village of Wharram Percy based on archaeological findings

Medieval villages were quite small, with the average population falling between 150 and 250 people. In some places, like Scandinavia, peasant homes lay far from one another instead of in a central location. During the High Middle Ages, many villages across Europe grew independently, without a central manor. In England, the manorial system continued to be common. Much of what is known today about the life of medieval peasants is preserved in records from England.

Most of the peasants on a manor were tenants who rented their land from the lord. Although they were tenants, however, they felt very strongly that the land they held belonged to them. Lords recognized this (in fact, they usually felt the same way about the lands granted them by their own overlords) and respected it. When a man died, his landholding passed to one of his sons, usually the oldest. In some places the land was divided up among all the sons, or shared as one large holding by all the sons. In most areas, if a man had no sons, a daughter could inherit his holdings. Whatever the arrangement, the important thing was to keep the land in the family.

In some areas, peasant **allods** were very common. An allod was a freeholding, land that no lord had any claim on. There were parts of Europe where it was possible for peasants to own allods at the same time as they held land from a lord. In other places, allods were nonexistent.

THE FREE AND UNFREE

Peasants were legally categorized as either unfree or free. These categories had to do with how much service was owed to the lord. Some manors had few if any free peasants. In the late thirteenth century, the English village of Elton had twenty-two free households and forty-eight unfree households (and twenty-eight others that were unclassified).

The unfree were known as serfs or **villeins** (vih-LANES). They were required to work the lord's land or perform other work for a certain number of days each week. The more land a villein held, the more labor he or she had to do. By the thirteenth century, however, many lords were accepting money instead of work from their serfs. The work still needed to be done, however, so the villeins' payments would be used to hire laborers for the demesne.

Serfs also owed the lord numerous fees, which varied from manor to manor. In general, there was an annual payment known as head money, which symbolized the serfs' bond to their lord. The lord could impose a tax known as **tallage** whenever he needed extra cash. When an unfree woman married, she, her father, or her husband had to pay the lord a fee called **merchet**. If her husband did not live on one of the lord's manors, an extra fine was added to this. Another fee was paid if a serf moved off the manor. This was supposed

A peasant pays his taxes in eggs, grain, and meat to an abbot outside a monastery.

to be paid every year after the serf left. When a villein died, the lord had to be given the family's best cow or sheep; sometimes the lord took a piece of furniture or other household item instead. There was yet another payment when a serf took over a landholding, whether he bought or inherited it. Serfs who wanted to become priests, monks, or nuns could not do so unless they paid a fine to the lord. Villeins also had to turn over agricultural products at particular times of year—for example, a certain number of chickens, eggs, or cakes of beeswax at Christmas and Easter.

To get flour to bake bread, a peasant would take his grain to the lord's mill. There, a beast of burden, like a donkey, would pull the heavy millstones to crush the grain.

The Countryside in Medieval Europe

Unfree peasants were required to grind their grain at the lord's mill; the miller kept a portion of the flour for the lord, as well as a portion for himself. This was hated by many peasants, so much so that they hid hand mills in their houses and secretly ground their own grain. Once the serfs had flour, they could bake their bread only in the lord's ovens. Again, many simply didn't eat bread, but instead boiled their grain into porridge. Villeins were also frequently required to keep their sheep in the lord's sheepfold for the winter—the lord then kept all of the sheeps' manure to fertilize the demesne, while the serfs had little fertilizer for their own fields.

Both free and unfree peasants paid the lord some form of rent for their land. Otherwise, free peasants owed the lord little labor and were exempt from all the fines and fees imposed on villeins. On the other hand, in most parts of Europe by the twelfth century, even a manor's free tenants were expected to be obedient to the lord, and they looked to him for protection just as the serfs did. A free peasant who moved off the manor, however, was no longer tied to its lord in any way, while villeins were bound to their lord no matter where they went, usually for life.

Not surprisingly, no one wanted the burdens and obligations of being a serf. We have many records of villeins going to court to try to prove that they were actually free; they almost never succeeded. There were other ways, however, to achieve freedom. In many places, a serf who moved to a town and lived there for a year and a day was automatically freed. During the twelfth and thirteenth centuries, peasants in England, France, Spain, and especially Germany were encouraged to settle in new areas and found new villages. They cleared forests and drained marshes to create farmland where there had never been any before. In return, these colonists were guaranteed freedom for themselves and their descendants. During the High Middle Ages, lords also became more willing to allow serfs to buy their freedom.

THREE CLASSES OF PEASANTS

Whether villagers were free or not, they generally fit into one of three classes. At the top of village society were the wealthiest peasants, who were always few in number. These people held between 40 and 100 acres (16 and 40 ha) of land, some of which they rented to their own tenants. In some places, such as Germany, one of these wealthier peasants might occasionally rise into the lower nobility. On the other hand, members of the lower nobility occasionally sank into this peasant class.

The largest group of peasants was made up of those who held 12 to 32 acres (4.8 to 13 ha). To support the average peasant family, 12 acres of land was just enough, at least in a good year. With 32 acres, the family would have surplus crops to sell.

The lowest class held no land at all, or too little to support a family. Cotters were peasants who had only a cottage and yard, or at most 1 acre (0.4 ha) or so. Most cotters and other peasants with little land worked as laborers for the lord or for other peasants. Some landless villagers, however, were able to make a living by practicing various crafts.

A village might have a number of craftspeople or tradespeople, such as blacksmiths, carpenters, shoemakers, weavers, dyers, tanners, millers, bakers, and butchers. These people were very important to the life of the village. They could be free or unfree, and some might practice their trades along with farming. Many women brewed and sold ale, and nearly all women spun, wove, and sewed cloth. Most of this cloth making was done to clothe the family, but sometimes women additionally earned wages for this work. Women also served the village as midwives and healers.

The Village Baker

Bakers were among the most important merchants in the medieval village. Most breads were baked with wheat, rye, or barley, which was ground by the miller. White bread was more expensive and could only be afforded by the wealthiest peasants. The loaves were baked in a large oven heated by a roaring fire.

Before baking a loaf, the baker was required to mark each loaf. The mark, which might be a flower, crescent, initial, cross, or other symbol, was the signature of which baker made the bread. In many parts of England, there was a system in place that regulated the price of bread based on its weight. Some bakers would try to cheat this system by mixing their flour with chalk or sawdust, or cooking iron bars into the loaves to increase their weight and value. If caught doing this, a baker might be placed in the village stocks with a loaf of bread hanging around his neck as punishment.

Besides the farmers and craftspeople, there were other residents of the typical village. The lord's demesne had a staff that included servants, plowmen, shepherds, a cook, a dairyman or dairymaid, and others. These people often settled on small holdings on the demesne. The parish priest and his assistants lived on land near the church.

Some people did not live in one particular village, instead spending their lives wandering from one place to another. These included traveling craftspeople, such as tinkers, and beggars. Most villages were wary of strangers. In some places, a villager who was caught with strangers or giving beggars food or lodging would be fined as punishment.

Spindles and Wheels

From ancient times through the Middle Ages, spinning was a common woman's chore. Its tools were very simple: the distaff, basically a longish forked stick; and the spindle, a short, thin stick with a round weight on the bottom. The unspun wool was wound around the distaff, which the spinner held in her left hand (the "distaff side"—a phrase that has also come to mean the mother's side of the family). With her right hand, the spinner drew the wool fibers and meshed their ends with thread that was already on the spindle. Then she gave the spindle a twist to set it spinning. As it spiraled down toward the ground, the spindle's motion stretched and twisted the wool, making a strong thread. When the thread was long enough, the spinner paused to wind it around the spindle, then drew out more wool and began again.

With distaff and spindle, women could take their spinning everywhere, and they usually did. They spun not only while they were relaxing around the hearth fire in the evenings, but also while they were engaged in other tasks in the yard and fields. In fact, they spun whenever their hands were not busy with something else. This was essential because it took a great deal of thread to weave enough cloth to make clothes for the entire family. Not surprisingly, most peasants got only one or two new outfits a year!

In the late thirteenth century, a new invention arrived on the scene in Europe. This was the spinning wheel, which may have originated in India or the Middle East. It took half as much time to spin thread on a spinning wheel as it did to spin the same amount of thread with a drop spindle. However, many years passed before the new invention was widely adopted, especially in the countryside. Hand spinning wool produced better quality thread than spinning with a wheel. Spinning wheels were expensive, too, and they could not be carried everywhere. So, for several centuries more, most peasant women continued to spin the old-fashioned way.

A woman, dressed as a common villager, feeds wool through a wooden spinning wheel in a medieval reenactment.

CHAPTER FIVE
ALL IN A
DAY'S WORK

Villagers plow and sow the field to
prepare for the new growing season.

"He who plows with oxen or any other animals beside the sown land of another, where wheat or any cereal, or leguminous crops are to be sown, must leave four furrows beside this sown land, so that, when he turns, he causes no damage. Whoever breaks this rule, shall be fined ten shillings, and will make good the damage he has done."

—a 1427 farming law from Montepescali, Italy

Farming formed the backbone of the medieval village. The peasant's life cycled around the seasons for planting and harvesting and raising livestock. Most merchants also relied on farming for their livelihood. They fashioned plowshares and hoes for working the land and prepared the grain and leather needed to feed and outfit livestock.

THE AGRICULTURAL YEAR

The greatest events of the work year were plowing, planting, and harvesting. These were all community efforts, during which the entire village pitched in to help. The way these tasks were done was strictly regulated by the village bylaws, which were made by the villagers themselves. For example, in Elton, "strangers" who were hired to help with the harvest were not allowed to carry any of the grain.

Plowing was done in both spring and fall to prepare the fields for planting. The fallow field was plowed in summer to keep down weeds. In a typical family, the husband guided the plow and his wife goaded the horses or oxen who pulled it. Most peasants could not afford to keep enough horses or oxen to pull a plow, so families combined their resources, sharing both animals and plows. After planting, the grain fields had to be weeded often. When harvest time came, every able-bodied person in the village took part in cutting, binding, and carting or carrying the sheaves of grain.

Peasant Women

Historians used to think that nearly all outdoor agricultural work was done by men, while women worked in the fields only during the harvest. Recent studies, however, have shown that women did a great deal more. They hauled manure to fertilize the fields, sowed seed, hoed, weeded, separated wheat from chaff, took part in haymaking, and carried grain to the mill. In regions where grape growing was important, women worked alongside men in the vineyards, pruning and tying vines. In some areas, such as southwestern France, all shepherds were men. In many other places, however, women tended not only sheep but also cows and oxen, geese and chickens, and pigs. Women's tasks included feeding, milking, shearing, and slaughtering the livestock in their care.

In peasant families, all household work was done by women and girls. They tended the hearth fire and carried water from the well. They spun and dyed wool, wove cloth, and made the clothes for everyone in the household. They raised vegetables in the croft and prepared all the family's meals. Other responsibilities included making butter and cheese, and preserving food for the winter. If a family was able to raise any extra food, it was often the wife who went to a market or fair to sell the surplus.

A Manual for Farming

During the early 1300s, an Italian scholar named Petrus de Crescentius wrote one of the most famous medieval texts on agriculture. Entitled *Ruralia Commoda*, the book is written in Latin. It is divided into twelve sections and offers a wealth of advice on how to properly run an estate, covering all kinds of tasks, from beekeeping to producing wine. The book also includes a monthly calendar of chores to be completed each month.

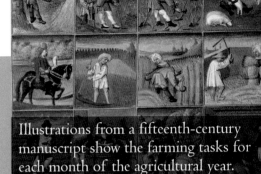

Illustrations from a fifteenth-century manuscript show the farming tasks for each month of the agricultural year.

The author also offers some peculiar advice, which includes:

- Cucumbers shake in fear during a thunderstorm.
- A crop of squash will fare well if planted in human ashes and watered with oil.
- Planting certain varieties of lettuce in a ball of goat manure will result in a tastier crop.

In most places, peasant women could legally both buy and inherit land. In one part of England, in the fourteenth century, 14 percent of the peasant landholders were women, most of them widows. All women landholders, free and unfree, were required to work their holdings and owed the lord the same rents and services as male landholders. We have records of many independent peasant women. One, for example, left her home village in southwestern France and bought a house, farm, and vineyard in another village. She kept a flock of sheep and dyed their wool to earn money. During harvest time, she and her children worked as hired laborers.

Although some peasant women enjoyed freedom and many of the same privileges as men, these instances were a rarity. Medieval society was largely patriarchal, with women considered to be beneath men.

CHAPTER SIX
FAMILY TIES

All members of a peasant family worked the land. Here, a mother and daughter gather stalks of wheat to be bound as sheaves.

"The most needy are ... poor folk in cottages, burdened
with children and the landlord's rent. What they save by
their spinning they spend it in house-hire, also in milk and
meal to make their porridge with, to fill their children who
cry for food. And they themselves suffer much hunger, and
woe in winter-time when they wake at night to rise to rock
the cradle ..."
—a description of a peasant woman's hardships, from
"Piers the Plowman," a fourteenth-century poem

The average medieval peasant household included a mother, father, children, and sometimes, members of the extended family. Among the peasant class, family ties ran deep. Each member of the family contributed to the successful running of the household. Women worked alongside their husbands and also oversaw the day-to-day tasks of the household, from raising the children to preparing the meals. Wealthier households might have had extra help from a servant or two.

Well-off peasant families generally included about five children. Poorer families were likely to have only two or three. Most households had a cat, to keep down rodents, and perhaps a dog or two, to guard the home and livestock. (In southern France, however, peasants tended to be highly suspicious of cats, regarding them as creatures of the devil.) These animals may often have been treated with affection, but most people probably thought of their cats and dogs more as working farm animals than as pets.

A peasant farmer leads his horse with his wife and child riding atop its back down a winding country road.

A COUNTRY UPBRINGING

All babies were born at home. Birth was a frightening and dangerous experience because there were not many medical techniques to help out if something went wrong. Also, no one in medieval Europe knew about germs, so no measures were taken to prevent infection. During labor, the mother-to-be was supported and comforted by two or three women friends and relatives. If she was lucky, an experienced midwife would also be there to help deliver the baby. Even with a midwife's care, however, many mothers and babies died either during or soon after birth.

If the mother lived, she normally breast-fed the child herself for one to two years. Otherwise, another village woman would have to nurse and care for the child. In real emergencies, peasants sometimes fashioned a makeshift baby bottle out of a cow's horn.

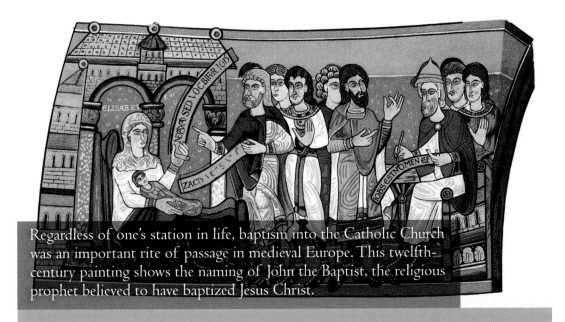

Regardless of one's station in life, baptism into the Catholic Church was an important rite of passage in medieval Europe. This twelfth-century painting shows the naming of John the Baptist, the religious prophet believed to have baptized Jesus Christ.

A Baby's Baptism

All babies were baptized, whether or not they lived. If an infant died during birth, the midwife would typically perform a short baptism. Babies that lived were promptly brought to church to be baptized and brought into the Christian faith. Mothers did not attend the baptism; they were not allowed into the church for some weeks after childbirth and had to go through a ceremony of purification first.

The midwife, father, and godparents would proceed to the church. In front of the church doors, a short ceremony took place, during which the priest blessed the child and placed salt in its mouth, then performed an exorcism to drive away any demons within the child. This was followed by more blessings and immersion in a font in the church itself.

Following the baptism, the baby was dressed in a white christening gown and anointed with myrrh, a holy oil. The godparents would make a commitment to the Christian faith on behalf of the infant. Once the baptism was complete, the celebration continued at home with gifts and feasting.

off, there might be long negotiations. The bride had to have a **dowry** of money, goods, or farm animals to bring to the marriage. The groom had to guarantee a **dower**, the portion of his property that would be his wife's if he died before she did. If the families were villeins, it was important to decide who would pay merchet to the lord.

Once everyone was satisfied, the couple became betrothed, or engaged. Since villages were small, the two usually already knew each other (noble couples often had never met before their wedding). Parents could not force their children to marry. Both the bride and the groom had to agree to the marriage for it to be legal.

Peasant weddings were very informal. Often the couple simply exchanged promises and a kiss in front of the church door. Sometimes they would then go into the church to attend **Mass**. After the ceremony, there would be a wedding feast to celebrate the new marriage. Some peasants, especially poor ones, were married in an even simpler ceremony, called a private marriage. The couple made their wedding vows to each other with no priest, friends, or family members present to witness. Even though such a marriage began in secret, the couple was considered legally married.

The newlyweds might move into a home of their own, or they might live with one of their families. If they lived on a holding belonging to the woman or her family, the husband often took his wife's last name. Even so, the husband was always regarded as the head of the family. Nearly all medieval thinkers, writers, and preachers agreed that men were superior to women. Villagers heard this viewpoint everywhere from sermons to jokes. Husbands were entitled to discipline their wives by hitting and even beating them. Women were expected to bear this treatment without complaining.

If a marriage was unhappy, peasant couples often separated. Sometimes they went through the process of getting a divorce, but sometimes they didn't bother, even if they wanted to remarry later. The second wedding might take place privately, or there might be a church-door ceremony in a neighboring village. As far as we know, none of this was particularly scandalous to medieval peasants.

Many members of the medieval village would join together to celebrate a peasant wedding, complete with lively music and feasting.

Village Life

One way or another, many peasant marriages ended up being full of affection and satisfaction for both partners. Marriage still did not last especially long, however. The average peasant could expect to live for only about another twenty years after getting married. Since husbands were usually ten or so years older than their wives, a large number of women became widows. A widow was free to remain unmarried if she wished, although her family or lord might try to pressure her into remarrying. If she held land, she owed the lord all the rents and services due on it. If she did not remarry, she either had to work the land herself or hire laborers to work it for her.

People were considered to be elderly when they reached age forty-five. In some places, their age made them more respected in their families and in the village. In other places, the elderly were less respected. In southwestern France, elderly women were held in high esteem and were asked for advice on a regular basis. On the other hand, people in northern Italy feared that an old woman's "evil eye" could harm babies.

A villager who was too old to continue working generally transferred his or her holdings to the person who would inherit the land, usually a son. In return, the heir promised to support the "retiree." Some aging peasants made arrangements with other villagers to support them. Another possibility was to buy a kind of pension plan from a monastery. This provided a room, food, drink, clothing, candles, firewood, and even, if the peasant could afford it, servants and a house with a garden and pasture.

When a villager was very ill, the priest was summoned to help him or her prepare for death. Two things were of the greatest importance to peasants on their deathbed: to be surrounded by their loved ones and to be assured that their souls were saved. After a person died, there was usually a day or two of keeping vigil over the body; these wakes often became merry, drunken parties. The body was washed and prepared for burial by the women of the family or neighborhood. In southwestern France, when the head of the household died, the family would keep some of his hair and fingernail clippings so that his good fortune would not desert the house.

Funerals were generally very simple. The body was sewn into or wrapped in a shroud, then laid on a bier and carried into the parish church. After a Mass was finished, the body was buried in the churchyard. Here, most medieval peasants believed, the dead person slept and awaited the Last Judgment.

From solemn rituals like funerals to joyous events like the arrival of a new baby and weddings, any occasion in the village drew the tightly woven community together.

CHAPTER SEVEN

FESTIVITIES, FUN, AND FOLKLORE

During some holidays, fortunate
villagers were invited to the manor
house for a sumptuous feast.

"Not the kalends [first day of the month] of May, nor the
leaf of a beech
Nor the song of a bird, nor a gladiolus
Can bring me enjoyment, my fine, gay lady,
Until I receive a message express
From your lovely person that will promise me
The new pleasures that love attracts me to
And it delights me and it leads me
To you, my true lady."
—an English translation of lyrics from "Kalenda Maya," a
May Day celebration song, written by the twelfth-century
French troubadour Raimbaut de Vaqueiras

The passing of time was very different for those living during the Middle Ages than it is for people today. For most peasants, the day began with the rising of the sun and ended at dusk. Their lives were very much tied to the cycles of farming. Instead of months they would speak of "the season when the elm leaves appear" or "the time of the turnip harvest."

The peasant year was also broken up by various Christian feast days: for example, the Nativity of the Virgin (September 8), All Souls' Day (November 2), and the Feast of **Saint** John (June 24). In fact, almost every day of the year was dedicated to a saint, an event in the life of Jesus, or an important religious concept. Usually the parish priest had a calendar, and he would tell villagers when important days were.

FESTIVE DAYS

Each season had at least one holiday when no work was done and the villagers were free to play games and feast. The greatest of all holidays was Christmas. Its celebrations lasted for twelve days. There were no Christmas trees, but people of all classes decorated their homes with holly, mistletoe, and other evergreens. On the manors, peasants owed the lord extra bread, eggs, and chickens. In some places, a few or all of the villagers were invited to a Christmas feast in the great hall of the manor house.

Since Jesus was born among animals in a stable, farm animals were often honored during the Christmas season. The first serving of some of the special Christmas foods was given to a favorite horse or cow, and then all the animals received extra helpings of feed. Besides commemorating the birth of Jesus, many peasants probably felt that their winter gift to the animals would help increase the strength and size of their herds and flocks in the spring.

The Christmas season ended with Epiphany, or Twelfth Night, which fell on January 6. On this day, peasants in many areas took cups of cider and small cakes out to the orchards. They would walk or dance around the trees, singing something like this:

> Hail to thee, old apple tree!
> From every bough
> Give us apples enow;
> Hatsful, capsful,
> Bushel, bushel, sacksful,
> And our arms full, too.

Then there was another festive meal. In some English villages, mummers, or amateur actors, would liven up the feast with traditional dances and plays. Often they acted out the story of Saint George and the dragon.

Easter week was celebrated with many games, often involving eggs (such as trying to roll an egg across the floor in a straight line). The lord of the manor usually received an extra payment of eggs from his tenants during this season. Once more, some villagers might be invited to feast at the manor house. The meal's main course was usually lamb or pork.

May Day was a joyous festival celebrated in much of northern and western Europe. It marked the beginning of summer and was celebrated with maypole dances and bonfires. On the eve of May Day, young people often stayed out in the woods all night. In the morning, they returned to the village with flowers and green boughs to decorate their homes. Often one of the village girls was crowned with a wreath of flowers and named queen of the May. Games and sports were played throughout the day, and the queen of the May gave the winners their prizes.

During a May Day celebration, peasants dance around a festively decorated maypole.

Saint George and the Dragon

During the Middle Ages, Saint George was one of the most widely honored Christian saints. He was said to have been a soldier who was born in Asia Minor during the late third century CE. A great many legends added to his story. In the most popular of these legends, Saint George went to Libya to fight a dragon. The dragon lived in a lake and had been gobbling down two sheep every day. When the nearby villages ran out of sheep, the people offered the monster maidens to eat instead. No army had been able to destroy the dragon. However, Saint George was able to kill it with a single blow, just as the beast was about to devour a young princess. The king of the land gave the saint a huge reward for rescuing his daughter and delivering the people from the dragon's awful rampages. Saint George divided this reward among the poor villagers, then rode off on further adventures.

In much of the British Isles, Lammas (August 1) was another occasion when villagers feasted at the manor house. This holiday celebrated harvest time. In some places, villagers would "sing the harvest home," all gathering for a songfest in the manor's great hall. At this time, too, loaves of bread and other farm products were offered and blessed in church.

There were many other holidays and Christian feast days. In addition, each village celebrated an annual feast in honor of the parish's patron saint. Many villagers would stay up, keeping a vigil, all through the night before this day. In the morning, they would go to hear a Mass especially in honor of their patron. For the rest of the day, there would be singing, dancing, storytelling, games, and wrestling matches, all frequently taking place in the churchyard.

THE SABBATH DAY

As on major holidays, the villagers were not expected to work on Sundays. Three church services were held on this day of rest, but most peasants went only to the midday Mass. Priests complained that it was often difficult to get people to attend church services at all. In fact, in some areas it was common for fewer than half the villagers to regularly go to church.

Mass was recited or sung by the priest. The words were in Latin, the official language of the Catholic Church. Few if any peasants understood Latin, and there was little congregational participation in the worship service. People often got restless and commonly chatted and flirted with one another during Mass. Some parish priests preached a sermon in the people's own language, at least once in a while. The sermon would explain biblical teachings, describe the lives of the saints, tell stories that illustrated Christian values, or urge the people to give up sinful practices (such as dancing in the churchyard!). Sometimes a wandering friar or monk would come to the village and preach a lively sermon either in the church or outdoors, generally attracting a large crowd.

SOCIALIZING AND STORYTELLING

Even on workdays, peasants didn't always labor from sunup to sundown. Whether in the fields or around the house, there was often time to take a break and gossip with a friend. Villagers frequently got together for company and conversation at dinnertime. After dinner, they might sit around the hearth fire and talk long into the night. As they discussed everything from religious beliefs to their neighbors' love lives, the women spun or sewed and the men mended tools. Some nights there would be singing and storytelling in addition to the pleasures of good conversation. Men and women alike also socialized in taverns. In most villages, the tavern was simply the home of someone who had recently brewed a batch of ale. In places like France and Italy, wine was more widely enjoyed than ale.

In this illustration from the 1500s, two archers demonstrate their prowess with a bow and arrow in front of an audience of peasants.

Games and sports were popular with both children and adults. Peasants played checkers, chess, and dice, as well as games like blind-man's buff. Wrestling, archery, and swimming were popular as well. Many people liked to watch cockfights, dogfights, and the like.

Sometimes traveling jugglers, musicians, storytellers, and other entertainers would come to a village. Along with the enjoyment they gave, they brought news and gossip from other areas.

HEROIC TALES

In the centuries before radio, television, and the Internet, storytelling was one of the most popular forms of entertainment. Some stories, called ballads, were in rhyme and set to music. Peasants usually had to tell their own stories and sing their own ballads. Their opportunities to hear professional entertainers were rare.

Many peasant stories were similar to the Grimms' fairy tales that are read to children today. The medieval versions of such tales, however, tended to be much more violent and realistic than ours. They reflected the harsh realities of peasant life. For example, in many of these stories, whenever the peasant heroes are offered any sort of magical gift or wish, all they want is food—good food, and plenty of it. To people who were often hungry and malnourished, hardly anything better could be imagined.

Peasants also liked to hear and tell stories about the great heroes of the past. In Ireland, some of the most popular tales were about Fionn MacCumhal (Finn MacCool), the head of an ancient band of warriors. Fionn and his men encountered giants, fairies, sorcerers, and fierce enemies in their adventures. Only men were allowed to tell these tales, but everyone enjoyed hearing them.

Welsh peasants told of King Arthur and the group of heroes that gathered around him. These Arthurian stories spread to France and

Fionn MacCumhal, the Irish folk hero, and his band of followers.

England and became incredibly popular all over Europe. French peasants also celebrated the deeds of Charlemagne, the ruler whose ninth-century empire stretched from France to Italy. In northern Italy, some medieval peasants even named their children after characters from the Charlemagne stories.

Peasants in Norway and Iceland told of their ancestors, the Viking raiders, explorers, and settlers of the ninth through eleventh centuries. They also enjoyed stories based on ancient legends about a dragon slayer, a warrior woman, and an enchanted ring. These tales were relished by German peasants, too.

The hero of many Spanish stories was El Cid. An eleventh-century military leader, El Cid fought both for and against the Muslims in Spain. He won renown not only for his bravery but also for his dedication to justice and his love for his wife and daughters.

Robin Hood, the most famous of all medieval peasant heroes, was not a warrior or king but an outlaw. He is still a popular character, but his story has changed a great deal since medieval times. When his adventures were first celebrated in northern England and southern Scotland during the thirteenth century, Robin Hood was a well-known robber and enemy of the English king. During the next few centuries, his reputation increased, until he became the noble thief, who stole from the rich to give to the poor, that we know so well today. And although Little John was an important character from the very beginning, Maid Marian did not become part of the Robin Hood legend until after the Middle Ages.

The Countryside in Medieval Europe

Robin Hood and the Monk

"Rhymes of Robin Hood" were popular with English peasants as early as the 1300s. The first of these rhymes to be written down, in 1450, was the ballad called *Robin Hood and the Monk*. This is a story about Robin Hood's visit to a Nottingham church on the holy day of Whitsun, or Pentecost, and his subsequent arrest and escape from prison. The poem portrays Robin's devotion to the Virgin Mary as well as his daring and the faithfulness of his "merry men." Here, adapted into modern English, are some stanzas from this popular medieval ballad:

> In summer, when the woods are bright,
> And leaves are large and long,
> It is full merry in the fair forest
> To hear the sweet birds' song,
>
> To see the deer draw to the dale
> And leave the hills so high
> And shade themselves beneath the leaves,
> Under the greenwood tree.
>
> So it befell upon Whitsun,
> Early in a May morning,
> The sun rose up shining fair,
> And the merry birds did sing.
>
> "A merry morning," said Little John,
> "By Christ that died on the tree!

There is no man merrier than I

In all of Christianity.

"Pluck up your heart, my dear master,"

Little John did say,

"And think how fair a time it is

In a morning of May!"

"Yet one thing grieves me," said Robin,

"And does my heart much woe:

That I may not on this holy day

To Mass or other service go.

"It is two weeks and more," said he,

"Since my Savior I have seen.

Today I will go to Nottingham,

With the might of the sweet Virgin."

Unfortunately, Robin and Little John quarrel, and so Robin goes off to Nottingham alone. While he is praying in church, a certain monk recognizes him and betrays him to the sheriff. After a short fight, Robin is arrested, but Little John is loyal still, and he uses trickery and strength to set Robin free. Soon the pair of outlaws are safely back in their forest home:

The sheriff made to search Nottingham,

Through every street and alley,

But Robin was in merry Sherwood,

Lighthearted as leaf on tree.

. . .

Thus John got Robin Hood out of prison —
It is certain, without a doubt.
When his men saw him safe and sound,
With gladness they did shout.

They poured out wine to celebrate,
Under the leaves so small,
And ate pastries filled with venison,
And washed them down with ale.

FAR-OFF PLACES

Travel, much more often than we might expect, was another way that people in the Middle Ages entertained themselves. Kings, along with their nobles and households, liked to make "progresses" through the countryside. Peasants went to fairs and markets in neighboring villages and towns. All sorts of people also went on **pilgrimages**, journeys to important religious sites. Pilgrimages were believed to be good for a person's soul, but they also provided an opportunity to see new places, meet new people, and experience new things.

Popular sites for pilgrimage included the shrine of Thomas à Becket in Canterbury, England; the shrine of Santiago de Compostela in Spain; and the holy cities of Rome (Italy) and Jerusalem (Israel).

Peasants on Pilgrimage

Geoffrey Chaucer, who lived from about 1340 to 1400, was one of the greatest writers in English literature. His most famous book is *The Canterbury Tales*, in which a group of people on a pilgrimage to the shrine in Canterbury entertain one another by telling stories. Four of the pilgrims are typical country dwellers: the Parson, the Plowman, the Miller, and the Reeve. Here, adapted into modern English, are Chaucer's descriptions of each of them:

The Parson

There was a good man of religion,

A poor parson of a small town,

Who Christ's gospel truly preached.

His parishioners he would devoutly teach.

He was good-willed and wondrously diligent,

And in adversity always patient.

…

His parish was wide, with houses far asunder,

But he never failed, in rain or thunder,

In sickness or in trouble, to visit

The farthest parishioners, well-off and not,

Going all on foot, in his hand a staff.

This noble example to his sheep he gave:

First he acted, and afterward he taught.

Out of the Gospel these words he caught:

"If gold rusts, what can iron do?"

For if a priest is foul, in whom we trust,

The Countryside in Medieval Europe

No wonder if a common man should rust!

. . .

To draw folk to heaven by fairness

And good example—this was his business.

. . .

The teachings of Christ and of the Twelve

Were what he taught—but first he followed them himself.

The Plowman

With the parson there was a plowman, his brother,

Who had hauled many a cartload of manure.

A good and honest laborer was he,

Living in peace and perfect charity.

He loved God best with his whole heart

At all times, whether life was easy or hard,

And next he loved his neighbor as himself.

He would thresh and also dig and delve,

For Christ's sake, for every poor creature,

Without any pay, if it lay in his power.

The Miller

The miller was a stout fellow for any occasion.

He was full big of muscle and also of bone:

That proved well, for everywhere he came

To wrestle, he would win the first-prize ram.

A painting by Henry Stacy Marks, an eighteenth-century artist, shows the Miller riding on horseback to Canterbury.

...

His beard was as broad as a digging spade.

Right on the tip of his nose he had

A wart, and upon it stood a tuft of hairs

As red as the bristles of a pig's ears.

His nostrils were black and wide.

He bore a sword and small shield at his side.

...

His mouth was as big as a wide furnace door.

He was a loud boaster and a rude joker—

His jests were of sin and ribaldry.

He could well steal grain, taking three times his fee—

He had a thumb of gold, by God.

He wore a white coat and a blue hood.

The Countryside in Medieval Europe

The Reeve

The reeve was a slender man with a **choleric** mood.

He shaved his beard as close as he could.

. . .

Well could he keep a storehouse and a bin—

No auditor could do him in.

He knew by dry weather and by the rain

How well the seed would yield the grain.

His lord's sheep, his cattle, his dairy,

His pigs, his horse, his stock, and his poultry—

All were wholly in this reeve's governing,

And on his honor he gave the reckoning.

. . .

There was no bailiff, no herder or other soul,

Whose tricks and cheating he did not know;

They were in dread of him as they were of death.

His dwelling was full fair upon a heath.

. . .

He was rich with all that he had stored.

Subtly could he please his lord,

Making gifts and loans from the lord's own goods,

And receive thanks from him, with a coat and hood.

In youth he had apprenticed with a master

To become a good craftsman, a carpenter.

CHAPTER EIGHT

TRIALS AND TRIBULATIONS

King Richard II prepares to meet the rebels leading the English Peasants' War.

"Never was any land or realm in such great danger as England at that time. It was because of the abundance and prosperity in which the common people then lived that this rebellion broke out … The evil-disposed in these districts began to rise, saying, they were too severely oppressed; ... [that their lords] treated them as beasts. This they would not longer bear, but had determined to be free, and if they laboured or did any other works for their lords, they would be paid for it."

—Jean Froissart on the Peasants' Revolt of 1381

Toward the end of the Middle Ages, a spirit of independence ignited in the peasant class, fueling their desire for change. But for much of the time period, life was certainly not easy. Bad harvests, deadly diseases, poor sanitation, and high taxes were just a few of the daily hardships they encountered.

Like farmers everywhere, medieval peasants were at the mercy of the weather. Constant, heavy rains could delay planting, cause already-planted seed to mold in the ground, flood seedlings, or ruin an almost-ripe crop. If there was not enough rain during the growing season, the crops would dry up. Hailstorms and early frosts were especially dreaded as harvest time approached.

Time was also the peasant's enemy, especially the serf's. There were only so many days when conditions were right for plowing, planting, and harvesting.

Villeins had to tend not only their own crops but also the lord's. In Elton, for most of the year, the serfs were required to work for the lord two days a week. In August, however, the requirement increased to three days, and in September—at the height of the harvest—to five. This left little time for serfs to tend their own land.

Peasant farmers were responsible for almost the entire food supply of medieval Europe, and yet peasants often had little to eat themselves. They frequently suffered from malnutrition. They ate meat rarely—sometimes only on major feast days—and had few other sources of protein. The variety of fruits and vegetables available to them might also be quite limited.

During this period, there were not many effective treatments for disease. Peasants' health was also threatened by poor sanitation. Not only was there no indoor plumbing, but even outhouses seem to have been almost unheard of. In some places, villagers commonly had huge piles of animal manure sitting right in their yards.

The demands of the lord caused additional hardship for a great many peasants. The numerous rents, fines, and fees owed to the lord could be a crippling burden for the poor. Strict limits were placed on how much firewood peasants could gather from the forests, and hunting by peasants was usually forbidden. Even if wolves, deer, or other creatures came out of the woods and destroyed the flocks or crops of the villagers, they still were not allowed to shoot at the animals. Villeins who were injured or seriously ill were given sick leave for up to a year, but after that they were required to return to work whether they were well or not. There were some peasants who ended up wandering from village to village, unable to support themselves except by begging.

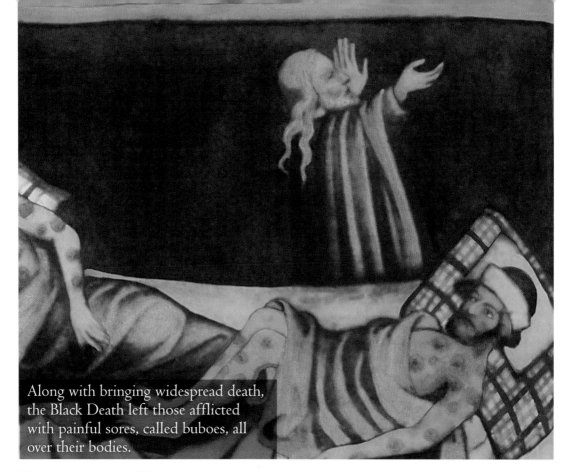

Along with bringing widespread death, the Black Death left those afflicted with painful sores, called buboes, all over their bodies.

DISEASE AND DISASTERS

In the fourteenth century, a series of disasters added to the routine hardships of peasant life. First came two years of extremely bad harvests, which led to widespread starvation. In England, this was followed by epidemics of typhoid fever and livestock diseases, but the worst was yet to come.

In 1348–1349, the Black Death, a devastating plague, swept through Europe. Rich and poor; young and old; cities, castles, villages, monasteries—no one could escape the disease. Children and the poor were most vulnerable. Many areas lost one-third to two-thirds of their population. After this first outbreak, the Plague struck six more times before 1420.

At the same time, the Hundred Years' War was raging between England and France. Peasants bore the burden of the higher and more frequent taxes imposed by the kings of both countries. Peasants were also drafted to fight in the armies.

The war was waged entirely in France, so French villagers suffered worst of all. Their homes, crops, and lives were threatened not only by the invading English soldiers but also by bands of French soldiers raiding for supplies.

Depopulation and heavy taxation severely weakened numerous villages, where holdings and houses stood empty for years. Land was now cheap, but labor was expensive. Prices for food and other necessities increased dramatically. Peasants demanded higher pay, and lords demanded higher rents and fees. Due to labor shortages, laws were passed to try to force peasants to remain on the manors and work, at whatever jobs they were ordered to, at the lower wages of the past.

Peasant uprisings had occurred from time to time since the early Middle Ages. In the second half of the fourteenth century, however, a spirit of rebellion exploded across Europe. There were peasant revolts in France, Flanders (modern Belgium), England, Germany, Spain, and Italy.

These revolts marked the start of a new era, in which manorialism and serfdom would soon be left to the pages of history books. The ideas of freedom embodied in the peasant revolts led to a much freer society across England in which the average person held the power to determine his or her own path and destiny, without having to answer to anyone but him or herself.

tallage

A tax that villeins had to pay to their lord. In some places, it was paid every year, and in other places, the lord could demand tallage whenever he wished.

toft

The yard of an English peasant house.

vassal

A noble who held land from a king or more powerful noble in exchange for military service and a pledge of loyalty.

villein (vih-LANE)

An unfree peasant; synonymous with serf.

Further Information

Books

Alcock, Nat, and Dan Miles. *The Medieval Peasant House in Midland England.* Oxford, UK: Oxbow Books, 2014.

Barter, James. *Life in a Medieval Village.* San Diego, CA: Lucent Books, 2003.

Cels, Mark. *Life on a Medieval Manor.* The Medieval World. New York: Crabtree Publishing, 2004.

Padrino, Mercedes. *Feudalism and Village Life in the Middle Ages.* New York: World Almanac Library, 2006.

Singman, Jerry L. *The Middle Ages: Everyday Life in Medieval Europe.* New York: Sterling, 2013.

Websites

British Library: Peasants and Their Role in Rural Life
www.bl.uk/the-middle-ages/articles/peasants-and-their-role-in-rural-life#
Learn about the important role of peasants in medieval Europe in this article from the British Library.

History of Britain: Changing Lives
timelines.tv/index.php?t=0&8e1
Watch short videos and explore the lives of medieval serfs and peasants in the British countryside.

Peasant Homes in Midland England
www.archaeology.co.uk/articles/peasant-houses-in-midland-england.htm
Read this interesting article about peasant homes that have survived for over five hundred years in the English Midlands.

FILMS

Medieval England: The Peasants' Revolt. Phoenix Learning Group, 2008.

Medieval Lives: Birth, Marriage, Death. RLJ Entertainment, 2014.

ORGANIZATIONS

Canadian Society of Medievalists
www.canadianmedievalists.ca/index.php?lang=en
The Canadian Society of Medievalists is an organization dedicated to medieval studies. The society publishes an annual journal, *Florilegium*, and hosts an annual conference for medieval enthusiasts.

The Medieval Academy of America
www.medievalacademy.org
As the largest medieval organization in the United States, the Medieval Academy of America focuses on all areas of life during the Middle Ages. The academy holds annual conferences, publishes research, and offers a student membership.

Source Notes

Chapter 1: A Divided Society

p. 7, Joliffe, John, ed and trans. *Frossairt's Chronicles*. New York: The Modern Library, 1968.

p. 8–9, "Domesday Book," retrieved from http://www.domesdaybook.co.uk/compiling.html

Chapter 2: A Country Manor

p. 11, "Manorial Management & Organization, c. 1275," retrieved from http://legacy.fordham.edu/halsall/source/1275manors1.asp

Chapter 3: Parts of a Medieval Village

p. 17, "The Dialogue Between Master & Disciple, on Laborers, c. 1000," retrieved from http://legacy.fordham.edu/halsall/source/1000workers.asp

Chapter 4: Village Life

p. 23, "Description of Wharram Percy Deserted Medieval Village," retrieved from http://www.english-heritage.org.uk/visit/places/wharram-percy-deserted-medieval-village/history/description/#Fn%208

Chapter 5: All in a Day's Work

p. 33, Speed, Peter. *Those Who Worked: An Anthology of Medieval Sources*. New York: Italica Press, 1997. p. 31.

Chapter 6: Family Ties

p. 37, Warren, Kate Mary, ed. *Langland's Vision of Piers the Plowman: An English Poem of the Fourteenth Century*. London: T. Fisher Urwin, 1895. p. 128.

Chapter 7: Festivities, Fun, and Folklore

p. 47, Wilhelm, James J., ed. *Lyrics of the Middle Ages: An Anthology*. New York: Routledge, 1990. p. 106.

p. 55–57, *Robin Hood and the Monk*, adapted by Kathryn Hinds.

p. 58–61, Chaucer, Geoffrey. *The Canterbury Tales*. Edited by Donald R. Howard. New York: New American Library, 1969. Excerpts adapted by Kathryn Hinds.

Chapter 8: Trials and Tribulations

p. 63, "Chronicles of Jean Froissart," retrieved from http://www.bl.uk/the-middle-ages/articles/peasants-and-their-role-in-rural-life

p. 67, "John Ball's sermon at Blackheath," retrieved from http://www.bbc.co.uk/radio4/history/voices/voices_reading_revolt.shtml

BIBLIOGRAPHY

Atkinson, Clarissa W. *The Oldest Vocation: Christian Motherhood in the Middle Ages*. Ithaca, NY: Cornell University Press, 1991.

Bloch, Marc. *Feudal Society*. Translated by L. A. Manyon. Chicago: University of Chicago Press, 1961.

Chaucer, Geoffrey. *The Canterbury Tales: A Selection*. Edited by Donald R. Howard. New York: New American Library, 1969.

Clark, Ethne. *The Art of the Kitchen Garden*. New York: Knopf, 1987.

Cosman, Madeleine Pelner. *Medieval Holidays and Festivals: A Calendar of Celebrations*. New York: Charles Scribner's Sons, 1981.

Coulton, G. G. *The Medieval Village*. New York: Dover, 1989.

Darnton, Robert. "Peasants Tell Tales: The Meaning of Mother Goose," in *The Great Cat Massacre*, edited by Robert Darnton, 9–72. New York: Basic Books, 1984.

Duby, Georges. *France in the Middle Ages 987–1460: From Hugh Capet to Joan of Arc*. Translated by Juliet Vale. Oxford, UK: Basil Blackwell, 1991.

Gies, Frances, and Joseph Gies. *Cathedral, Forge, and Waterwheel: Technology and Invention in the Middle Ages*. New York: HarperCollins, 1994.

———. *Life in a Medieval Village*. New York: Harper & Row, 1990.

———. *Women in the Middle Ages*. New York: Barnes & Noble, 1978.

Halsall, Paul. "Internet Medieval Sourcebook." http://www.fordham.edu/halsall/sbook1.html.

Heer, Friedrich. *The Medieval World: Europe 1100–1350*. Translated by Janet Sondheimer. New York: World Publishing, 1961.

Herlihy, David, ed. *Medieval Culture and Society*. New York: Walker, 1968.

Herlihy, David. *Women, Family, and Society in Medieval Europe: Historical Essays, 1978–1991*. Oxford, UK: Berghahn Books, 1995.

Knight, Stephen, and Thomas H. Ohlgren. *Robin Hood and Other Outlaw Tales*. Kalamazoo, MI: Western Michigan University for TEAMS, 1997.

Le Roy Ladurie, Emmanuel. *Montaillou: The Promised Land of Error*. Translated by Barbara Bray. New York: George Braziller, 1978.

Luria, Maxwell S., and Richard L. Hoffman, editors. *Middle English Lyrics*. New York and London: W. W. Norton, 1974.

Packard, Sidney R. *12th Century Europe: An Interpretive Essay*. Amherst, MA: University of Massachusetts Press, 1973.

Shahar, Shulamith. *The Fourth Estate: A History of Women in the Middle Ages*. Translated by Chaya Galai. London and New York: Methuen, 1983.

TEAMS Middle English Texts. http://128.151.244.128/camelot/teams/tmsmenu.htm.

Tompkins, Ken. "Wharram Percy, the Lost Medieval Village." http://loki.stockton.edu/~ken/wharram/wharram.htm.

INDEX

Page numbers in **boldface** are illustrations. Entries in **boldface** are glossary terms.

Richard II, **62**, 67
Robin Hood, 54–57
Ruralia Commoda, 35

saint, 47, 49–51
sanitation, 18, 20, 63–64
schools, 41
serf, 7, 13, 24–25, 27–28, 40, 63–64, 66
    See also villein
sheep, 12, 17, 25, 27, 34–35, 50
sheepfold, 19
sokeman, 8
spindle, 30
spinning, 30, **31**
steward, 11–12, 14

tallage, 24
taxes, 8, 12–13, 24–25, **25**, 63, 65–67
tenants, 23, 27–28, 49
toft, 18
trestle table, 18
Tyler, Wat, 67

vassal, 7, 9
villein, 24–25, 27, 42, 64
    See also serf

waterwheels, 21, **21**
wells, 18, 34, 40
William the Conqueror, 8–9
windmills, 21
women, 9, 11, 15, 18, 24, 28, 30, 34–35, 37–38, 41–42, 44–45, 51